ON REVOLUTION

"It is in the nature of revolution, the overturning of an existing order, that at its inception a very small number of people are involved. The process in fact, begins with one person and an idea, an idea that persuades a second, then a third and a fourth, and gathers force until the idea is successfully contradicted, absorbed into conventional wisdom, or actually turns the world upside down. A revolution requires not only ammunition, but also weapons and men willing to use them and willing to be slain in the battle. In an intellectual revolution, there must be ideas and advocates willing to challenge an entire profession, the establishment itself, willing to spend their reputations and careers in spreading the idea through deeds as well as words."

Jude Wanniski, 1936-2005
The Way the World Works, (Touchstone Books, 1978)

THE FOUR YEAR CAREER®

SECOND EDITION

HOW TO MAKE YOUR DREAMS OF FUN AND FINANCIAL FREEDOM COME TRUE

OR NOT ...

BY
RICHARD BLISS BROOKE

ISBN # 0–9700399–2–1
Published by High Performance People, L.L.C.
1875 North Lakewood Drive
Coeur d'Alene, ID 83814
Telephone 888.665.8484, Fax 888.665.8485
Printed in the United States of America

10 9 8 7 6 5 4 3 2 1

AN INTRODUCTION FROM RICHARD BROOKE

As the author of this book I am biased. In 1977 I had my own four year career under my belt at Foster Farms, the single largest chicken processing plant in the world. With only 36 years to go I changed course and at the age of 22, I joined the ranks of the Network Marketing profession. It took me three years to make a living at it. I quit 100 times my first year and watched thousands quit who joined before, during, and after me.

Then I figured something out—and three years later I had 30,000 active partners building the business with me. Sure people still failed and quit but 30,000 people stuck with it. I was earning $40,000 a month in 1983 at the age of 28. I have earned millions since and have coached tens of thousands to earn $500 to $5,000 to $50,000 a month and more.

I figured out how to make Network Marketing work. So have a lot of other people.

Thirty-six years later, I have seen thousands of companies come and go and hundreds of thousands of hopeful Distributors quit before they made it ... or maybe they would have never made it. I have seen our profession dirty its pants with its own greed, selfishness, immaturity and general lack of character within its leaders. I have heard all the rational experiences and factoids about how and why this profession is the scourge of the earth. Many of those perspectives are right on, well deserved and make total sense.

I have also seen that, for those people who "figure it out," their lives are forever enriched financially, physically, emotionally and spiritually. Some would say that those who succeed in Network Marketing is "not fair." I would say that everyone who "takes a look" at Network Marketing as a part-time income or a significant wealth building alternative has the same opportunity to succeed. Life is not fair if you define fairness as "everyone wins." My mentors never promised me life would be fair. They just promised me it would "be." The rest was up to me.

In 2012, I would have been retiring from Foster Farms had I stuck it out. Not a bad thing. I loved the people there and even enjoyed the work. Just different.

Instead, I have traveled to every state in our union at least twice, every province and territory of Canada, over 20 fascinating countries (including Cuba three times), built incredible relationships with thousands of people from all over the world, had incredible successes as well as my share of bending failures. My favorite people in the world are still my high school buddies and my favorite place in the world is still home. I am grateful to be able to clearly make that distinction.

I suppose a person can figure out how something won't work or figure out how it will. Each intention produces a result.

SUCCESS

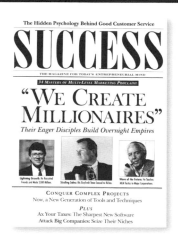

The Hidden Psychology Behind Good Customer Service

SUCCESS

THE MAGAZINE FOR TODAY'S ENTREPRENEURIAL MIND

34 MASTERS OF MULTI-LEVEL MARKETING PROCLAIM:

"WE CREATE MILLIONAIRES"

Their Eager Disciples Build Overnight Empires

CONQUER COMPLEX PROJECTS
Now, a New Generation of Tools and Techniques

PLUS
Ax Your Taxes: The Sharpest New Software
Attack Big Companies: Seize Their Niches

In March 1992, *SUCCESS* magazine featured the Network Marketing industry's skyrocketing success as its lead story. It was the first time a mainstream publication had done so in the industry's 50-year history. That is your favorite chicken chopper turned CEO, Richard Bliss Brooke, in the middle picture. (You can read about how they picked him in *Mach II With Your Hair On Fire.*) It outsold every issue in the 100 year history of the magazine.

Richard Bliss Brooke is a 35-year veteran of the Network Marketing profession, a member of the Board of Directors of the Direct Selling Association, a senior member of the DSA Ethics Committee and holder of many other accolades, including:

- Author of *The Four Year Career* and *Mach II With Your Hair On Fire, The Art of Vision and Self Motivation*
- Full-time Network Marketing Leader since 1977
- Owner of two Network Marketing companies
- Industry Expert and Advocate
- Motivational Seminar Leader
- Ontologist Coach

TABLE OF CONTENTS

CHAPTER 1

A Four Year Career vs. A Forty Year Career?

Security is mostly a superstition. It does not exist in nature, nor do the children of men as a whole experience it. Avoiding danger is no safer in the long run than outright exposure. Life is either a daring adventure, or nothing.

— Helen Keller

A Four Year Career vs. A Forty Year Career?

The 40/40/40 Plan

Since the dawn of the Industrial Revolution, over 250 years ago, the idea of a career has been to: work 40 hours a week for 40 years for 40% of what was not enough even for the first 40 years.

1. Get a good education ... a four year degree is your ticket.
2. Get a good job with a big company ... lots of benefits.
3. Work it for at least 40 hours a week, for 40 years to retire and enjoy the Golden Years.

Things have changed a lot since then. Your "company" is more likely to file bankruptcy to avoid paying your retirement than it is to honor it. Even states, counties and cities are starting to face the fact that they over promised and can't deliver. And even if the retirement is there ... even if your 401k is not a 201c, there is rarely enough retirement income from this model to have a gay ol' time in your Golden Years. Most people just hunker down and run out the clock. I don't know. Maybe they think this is a trial run and they get another shot at it.

Investing in Your Future

Tech companies today are paying kids ... 16–20 year olds, to "pass on college" and get in here and create products with us *now*.

All things being equal, college is still smarter than no college. But some kids are figuring out if they invest those four full-time years with $50,000–$500,000 towards their business ideas and talents, they can end up hiring a lot of college graduates. Think Bill Gates, Steve Jobs, and Larry Ellison.

The cheese has been cut up in a lot of different pieces and placed in different places. There is a big piece of it over here in Network Marketing.

The Four Year Career Alternative

Can you actually work at something for four years and have it provide everything you want in life for the next 40 years?

Well, yes, it is possible. But do most people? No. Most people do not build a Network Marketing empire in four years and enjoy a fabulous life from then on.

But they could. This book is about the "could," not the "should" or the "absolute." Just the "could."

First we need to understand it … not from rumor, not from Uncle Bob and his train wreck in Network Marketing 20 years ago. But understand the facts, just like we understand how succeeding at getting a job works.

Then we need to find something about the process that appeals to us. Maybe it is the upside to earn a king's ransom, maybe it is the freedom to work from home, maybe the flexibility to choose your own schedule, maybe to live/work from anywhere you choose or maybe it is the spiritual, leadership, communication and relationship building skills you will learn. You have to have a really good reason to take a road less traveled or it is too dark and scary.

Third, you need to learn to believe that it will work for you and those you offer it to. This takes time but it is the most important aspect of "figuring it out." Belief does not come from success. Success comes from belief.

Investing in Your Future

The rules most of us grew up with have consistently been thrown out the window over the past 30 years. Loyalty to one particular job no longer provides security. A four-year degree might get you a job, but that's about it. The average person today will change jobs seven to 10 times in their lifetime. Most will not end up settling in the careers for which they majored in college.

Saving and investing won't start to happen for most people until their kids are out of college—when most adults are well into their fifties. Starting to invest at age 50 only leaves about 20 years for accumulation. As we can clearly see from the compounding chart on the next page, it is not so important *how much* you invest, but for *how long* you invest.

Take a close look at the compounding chart for a reality check. Invest $500 a month at 7% from age 30 to 70 and you will have over $1.2 million. How much would you need to invest to end up with the same amount if you wait until you are 50?

In order to achieve the same cash value in only 20 years (starting at age 50 through 70), your required monthly investment is nearly

$2,500. That's almost five times the monthly investment needed than if you started at age 30!

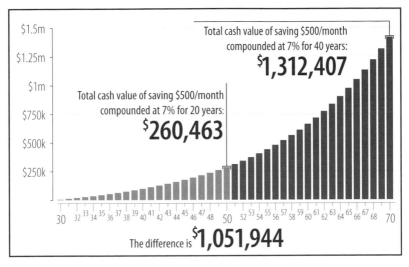

And notice I used a 7% return. That is quite a generous assumption.

The Investment Strategy

What about investment strategies? The models for us to choose from have traditionally been real estate and equities.

Liquid Investments/Equities
Most of us probably do this to some extent. We take what we can or will out of our paychecks, after paying taxes and all of our bills. If we are fortunate and/or frugal, we might end up with 10% to invest.

This system does work when we work it. We need to invest consistently, every month, and we need to invest in ways that produce at least a conservative return over time, such as 7%. Anyone of us who started doing this from our first working years would end up with a sizable nest egg. For those who waited, the results are less favorable. And equities can go from 100% to *zero* overnight if you pick the wrong investment such as Enron, Global Crossings, MCI, AIG, Bear Stearns, Washington Mutual, IndyMac, Goldman Sachs, Kodak, Hostess, General Motors, SAAB, American Airlines, MF Global, Borders, Solyndra, Lehman Brothers, Delta Airlines, WorldCom, Inc., etc.

Real Estate

Many of us gain most of our net worth through the payments we make over time on our own home. This works because we must pay someone for a place to live; therefore we are consistent with the investment. In higher-end markets and any waterfront community, historically the return is much more than 6%. However, we have also seen market corrections that have *dropped* real estate values by up to 50% even in those coveted California and Florida markets.

The Challenge

For most people who consider these strategies, it is deciding what to invest in, and, more importantly, where to get the money to invest. These strategies work great if you have the extra $1,000 a month to invest every month without fail for 25 years. Without it, you are a spectator. Are you tired of being a spectator? Do you know anyone else who is?

CHAPTER 2

WHY NETWORK MARKETING?

Far better it is to dare mighty things, to win glorious triumphs,
even though checkered by failure, than to take rank with those
poor spirits who neither enjoy much nor suffer much, because they
live in the gray twilight that knows neither victory nor defeat.

— THEODORE ROOSEVELT

Why Network Marketing?

There is a third strategy that anyone can employ to build extraordinary wealth and financial freedom, regardless of age, experience, education, income level or social status: Residual Royalty Income.

A Residual Royalty Income Offers Huge Advantages

1. You can build it part-time, any time.
2. You can build it from anywhere, any city, any virtual office.
3. You can launch it for $500–$1,000.
4. You are "in business" for yourself, but not *by* yourself, meaning your host company will do all the heavy investing and lifting and the team you join has a significant vested interest in you succeeding.
5. You can create enough tax deductions alone each year to make it worthwhile.
6. You can learn it while you earn it. You can create cash flow your first month.
7. You can earn an extra $500, $1,000, $5,000 or more a month—every month—to invest in the traditional options of real estate and equities.
8. And the most valuable and lucrative benefit is that of *Residual Royalty Income* and its asset value. Built in the right company—one that has proven it pays over the long haul—that income can, and should, be there forever.

The asset value of your Network Marketing income will be approximately 200 times your monthly income. If you are earning $5,000 a month in Residual Royalty Income, and you can rely on it continuing, your Residual Royalty Income could be worth $1 million.

How much would you have to earn to invest enough to build $1 million in real estate or equities? How long would it take? How much would you have to sacrifice in your *lifestyle* to do it?

It is 200 times easier to build your net worth all three ways, using your Network Marketing income to fund the other two options. And you can get to your target net worth in five to 10 years, versus it taking your whole lifetime.

Yeah But Why Network Marketing . . . Let's Start With a Couple of Simple Facts

Fact #1:
It's legal.

In the U.S. and around the world in over 70 countries, Network Marketing has been legally used for product distribution and compensating Distributors for more than 50 years.

During this time, Network Marketing has repeatedly been upheld by the federal and state courts as a legal distribution and compensation method, when the following legal guidelines are followed:

1. The main objective of the business is selling viable products or services at a market driven price. Meaning, there is a market for the product from consumers absent of the financial opportunity.
2. Potential incomes can't be promised. Even hypothetical incomes can't be inferred without the appropriate disclaimers.
3. Distributors are not paid (head hunting fees) for the act of recruiting others. Income has to come entirely from the sale of products.

There are many products or services that Distributors will be "customers" for as long as there is a financial opportunity to go with it. The means justify the end. Unfortunately, when all the shine wears off, no one continues to use the product. This is a pyramid scheme. The true test of a legitimate Network Marketing company is whether most of the product is sold to consumers who are not earning any commissions or royalties from the opportunity. Most Network Marketing Distributors start out pursuing the income opportunity but once they give up they settle in to being a customer. Most companies total sales are made up of these "wholesale" customers. Maybe they sell enough to get "theirs for free." This is easily 90% of most Network Marketing sales forces. The other 10% is made up of those earning a few hundred a month. Less than 1% build a sales force of these users and sellers such that they qualify for *The Four Year Career.*

The concept attracts very dynamic promoters—some are ethical, some not. Many Network Marketing companies have crossed the line legally and have been the subject of negative media, as well as civil and criminal penalties.

Fact #2:
Most companies fail, some succeed.

There are an estimated 2,000 Network Marketing firms distributing over $30 billion a year in goods and services in the U.S. alone. Only 260 of those are Direct Selling Association members. There are very few legitimate and successful companies that are not DSA members. The $30 billion number comes from members and public companies that report their sales. Most of those 2,000 companies never report their sales and go in and out of business as fast as in any other industry. Amway, Herbalife, Mary Kay Cosmetics, Forever Living Products, Nu Skin and Primerica each boast over $1 billion annually in sales, and have been in business and growing steadily for 30 to 50 years. Hundreds more sell between $10 million and $1 billion a year through millions of independent brand representatives.

As you can see from these numbers, most companies fail and they do so relatively quickly (within 12–24 months) and are quickly replaced by a dozen more attempting to attract the hearts and minds of a few sales leaders who might lead them to the geometric growth of prosperity. Most restaurants fail. Most dry cleaners fail. Most companies we went to work for just out of college or high school have already failed. It is the nature of free markets and enterprise.

Fact #3:
Most Distributors give up long before they could have succeeded.

Some individual Distributors have earned and enjoyed long-standing Residual Royalty Income fortunes of $1 million or more per year, for years. Many more earn from $1,000 to $10,000 a month.

Most individuals who pursue building a Network Marketing business, however, give up before they see the level of success for which they hoped.

The *average* Network Marketer never creates enough success to warrant doing anything beyond buying product at wholesale.

The fact is, people with *average* ambition, commitment and effort usually don't do well in a business like Network Marketing.

Is that the fault of the system or the individual? Both I think. Network Marketing is not easy. Who do you know who is not already involved and is looking to get involved? No one. We have a long way to go in educating the public and treating the public with respect and honor before there will be a public demand for our profession. To be successful, one must have a high level of personal confidence love talking to people be comfortable creating new relationships every day be coachable and most importantly be a proud ambassador of the Network Marketing profession. This book is designed to help move you along in that regard.

The person with "average" confidence, credibility, self esteem, ambition and promotional skills rarely earns more than enough to pay for their own product from the company they represent. In a few days, weeks or months they give up on the opportunity BUT if the product they represent has captured their loyalty they will remain a "member customer" oftentimes just earning enough to get their product for free. This model may make up the bulk of all sales volume for most companies.

Fact #4:
It's a major player in the global economy.

The Network Marketing method of marketing as an industry has grown 17 out of the last 20 years, including over 90% in just the past 10 years. A staggering *$110 billion* worth of goods and services are sold worldwide each year in this industry.

$10.9 billion

$9.2 billion

$3 billion

$2.9 billion

$2.7 billion

$2.5 billion

$2.3 billion

$2.2 billion

$1.7 billion

$1.5 billion

BELCORP

$1.3 billion

PRIMERICA

$1.3 billion

Fact #5:
It's growing.

Each week, about 475,000 people worldwide become sales representatives for one of these companies. That's *175,000 each week* in the U.S. alone.

There are 15 million Americans and 67 million people worldwide who participate at some level in this concept.

Twenty-five years ago there were no books written on the subject of Network Marketing. Now there are dozens … some have sold in the millions of copies. Fifteen years ago no mainstream magazines or newspapers or television shows had featured the positive uplifting opportunity of Network Marketing. Now there are hundreds of examples. Ten years ago there were virtually no "thought leaders" who endorsed our profession. Now most all of them do.

There are thousands of companies and millions of sales representatives … each looking to build their team. This is an idea whose time has come. And it is about to explode … in a good way.

It Works

The bottom line is, Network Marketing works and has worked to build extra—to extraordinary—individual wealth for more than 100 years. Some of the smartest people in the world are taking advantage of it.

Paul Zane Pilzer, World-Renowned Economist and Best-Selling Author of *The Next Millionaires*

> "From 2006 to 2016, there will be 10 million new millionaires in the U.S. alone … many emerging from Direct Selling."

Robert T. Kiyosaki, Author of *Rich Dad Poor Dad* and *The Business of the 21st Century*

> "… Direct Selling gives people the opportunity, with very low risk and very low financial commitment to build their own income—generating assets and acquiring great wealth."

Stephen Covey, Author of *The Seven Habits of Highly Effective People*

> "Network Marketing has come of age. It's undeniable that it has become a way to entrepreneurship and independence for millions of people."

Bill Clinton, Former U.S. President

"You strengthen our country and our economy not just by striving for your own success but by offering opportunity to others ..."

Tony Blair, Former British Prime Minister

"[Network Marketing is] a tremendous contribution to the overall prosperity of the economy."

David Bach, Author of the New York Times Bestseller, *The Automatic Millionaire*

"... you don't need to create a business plan or create a product. You only need to find a reputable company, one that you trust, that offers a product or service you believe in and can get passionate about."

Tom Peters, Legendary Management Expert and Author of *In Search of Excellence* and *The Circle of Innovation*

"... the first truly revolutionary shift in marketing since the advent of 'modern' marketing at P&G and the Harvard Business School 50 to 75 years ago."

Zig Ziglar, Legendary Author and Motivational Speaker

"... a home-based business offers enormous benefits, including elimination of travel, time savings, expense reduction, freedom of schedule, and the opportunity to make your family your priority as you set your goals."

Jim Collins, Author of *Built to Last* and *Good to Great*

"... how the best organizations of the future might run – in the spirit of partnership and freedom, not ownership and control."

Seth Godin, Best-Selling Author of *Permission Marketing, Unleashing the Ideavirus* and *Purple Cow*

"What works is delivering personal, relevant messages to people who care about something remarkable. Direct Sellers are in the best position to do this."

Donald Trump, Billionaire Businessman and Owner of the Trump Network

"Direct Selling is actually one of the oldest, most respected business models in the world and has stood the test of time."

Ray Chambers, Entrepreneur, Philanthropist, Humanitarian and Owner of Princess House

> "The Direct Selling business model is one that can level the playing field and close the gap between the haves and have-nots."

Roger Barnett, New York Investment Banker, Multi-Billionaire and Owner of Shaklee

> "… best-kept secret of the business world."

Warren Buffet, Billionaire Investor and Owner of three Direct Selling/Network Marketing companies

> "The best investment I ever made."

CHAPTER **3**

NETWORK MARKETING MYTHS

Every man takes the limits of his own field
of vision for the limits of the world.

— ARTHUR SCHOPENHAUER

NETWORK MARKETING MYTHS

Myth #1:
Getting in on the ground floor is the best way to success in a Network Marketing Company.

The truth is, it is the worst time to join. Ninety-five percent of all companies, including Network Marketing companies, go out of business in their first five years. Of course, no company is going to tell you that in their promotional materials. Everyone involved at the start of any company hopes it will succeed.

Another risk with a new company is that no company has its best foot forward early on. It takes years to develop competent, experienced staff, reliable procedures and efficient services.

The best time to join a Network Marketing company is usually when it is at least five years old, or backed by a larger company. By then, it has demonstrated a commitment and ability to:

- Grow ethically.
- Stay in business.
- Honor its Distributors and customers.

And yet, this allows you the opportunity to get involved with the company before they are so well-known that everyone has either already given them a try, or decided they aren't interested.

Myth #2:
Network Marketing is an opportunity for someone who is not doing well financially to make some money—maybe even a lot of money.

Unfortunately, many of the success stories have perpetuated this myth with a rags-to-riches theme. Although there are enough people to substantiate the myth, it is still a myth.

The same skills it takes to succeed in any marketing business are required in Network Marketing:

- You must be assertive.
- You must have confidence.
- You must be dynamic in your ability to express yourself.
- You must have enough resources to propel yourself through the challenges.

Those resources should include working capital, contacts, time, discipline and a positive, crystal-clear vision of where you intend to go with your business—whether it is easy or not.

The truth is that many people who are struggling financially are doing so for a number of reasons, including low self-esteem and/or lack of the basic skills and preparation that allow one to succeed in anything. Network Marketing is a powerful and dynamic economic model, but not so powerful that it can overcome peoples' lack of readiness or persistence.

The fact is that the people who are already successful in whatever they do, tend to also succeed in Network Marketing. The great part is, they are apt to do better financially in Network Marketing because the economic dynamics are so powerful. Successful people are rarely in a profession where they can earn on the leverage of thousands of other people. Real estate agents, teachers, coaches, medical professionals, counselors, small business owners, beauty professionals and physical fitness professionals may be stellar performers in their domain but how do they create the opportunity to earn on the efforts of thousands of others in their same profession? Here they can.

Myth #3:
Network Marketers succeed by being in the right place at the right time. Luck is a big factor.

Network Marketing is a business; it is not a hobby, a game, a scheme, a deal or something in which to dabble. People who treat it lightly do not succeed. People who treat it as a new career, a profession and a business have a reasonable opportunity to make it pay off very well. Professionals who treat it as a Wealth Building Art to be "mastered" eventually can earn a yacht load of money. Most people invite a few people to look and then quit. Those who master it invite a few people every day for a year or two and sometime in that "practice" they hone the art of listening more than talking, interpret rejection in a learning way, and learn how to craft their offer in such a worded way that someone actually WANTS to hear more. Just like any worthwhile career it takes time, patience and repetition.

The book *Outliers* brilliantly suggests that mastery of any worthwhile art requires about 10,000 hours of actual practice. That's two hours a day, six days a week, 50 weeks a year for guess how many years? The Four Year … Career.

Myth #4:
The way Network Marketing works is the "Big Guys" make all their money off the "Little Guys."

The "big guys, little guys" myth is usually perpetuated by people who define fairness as "everyone gets the same benefit, regardless of their contributions." That is how socialism works, not how Network Marketing works.

In Network Marketing, the people who attract, train and motivate the most salespeople earn the most money.

There are basically three levels of participation:

Wholesale Customer
This is someone who gets involved just to use the products and buy them at the same price that higher-volume Distributors would pay. This often requires a little higher minimum order and an annual renewal fee, very much like being a member of Costco or Sam's Club. Many Distributors end up just being wholesale customers after pursuing the income opportunity and deciding it is not for them.

Retailer
A retailer is a Distributor who focuses their efforts on just selling the products. In many cases they do not understand the income

opportunity well enough to sell *it* as effectively as they can sell the product.

A retailer will earn 20 to 50% commission on their own personal sales, and the upper limit of their income will usually be in the hundreds of dollars a month.

Network Marketing Leader

A Network Marketing leader is someone who is a wholesale customer, a retailer *and* someone who understands the income opportunity well enough to add selling *it* to their mix.

A Network Marketing leader may enroll as many as 100 people to build with them; sometimes two to three times that many. Out of the hundreds enrolled, most will just use the product; some will just retail it, and a very few will actually do what the Network Marketing leader did by enrolling many themselves.

To be a successful Network Marketing leader, one must be able to enroll lots of people to sell with them, and they must be able to train and motivate the group to continue growing. The better one is in these roles, the more money one will earn.

In simple terms, if a person sells a little and enrolls just a few people, they will earn far less than someone who sells a lot and enrolls, motivates and trains a group that grows. That's basic capitalism, which most North Americans consider quite fair.

Myth #5:
You have to use your friends and family to make any money in Network Marketing.

The truth is, you do not and you should not. Your friends and family should only become a part of your business if it serves them to do so. If it serves them—if they see an opportunity for themselves just like you did—then they are not being used, they are being served. If you do not believe your opportunity can serve them, do not offer it to them.

An opportunity that truly inspires *you* will most likely inspire them as well. Offer it to them. If they say no, respect and honor their viewpoint and do not make a nuisance of yourself.

Myth #6:
If Network Marketing really worked, everyone would get involved and the market would be saturated.

The truth is, although this is mathematically possible, history has proven that saturation is not an issue. There are many companies you will see featured in this book that have been in business for 30–50 years doing billions a year in business with millions of sales reps. Yet you are not one of them. Nor are 298 million people in the U.S. and 6.9 billion people worldwide.

Plus you might consider a great leader who personally sponsored 12 people 2,000 years ago. They have all been recruiting via weekly opportunity meetings and one-on-one for all of those 2,000 years. And yet most of the world does not subscribe to their program.

CHAPTER 4

TRADITIONAL SALES VS. NETWORK MARKETING

Many people fear nothing more terribly than to take a position which stands out sharply and clearly from the prevailing opinion. The tendency of most is to adopt a view that is so ambiguous that it will include everything and so popular that it will include everybody...

— MARTIN LUTHER KING, JR.

TRADITIONAL SALES VS.
NETWORK MARKETING

Most of us grew up with a traditional selling paradigm. It sounds like this ... if you're offered a product and the opportunity to earn money by selling that product, the amount of money you make will be based on the quantity of product that you personally sell.

In the Traditional Selling Paradigm, if you had a goal of selling $1 million worth of product a month, you might hire 100 full-time, professional salespeople to work for you, giving them each a territory and a quota of $10,000 in sales per month. If they couldn't meet that quota, of course, you would fire them and find other salespeople who could.

While Network Marketing is a form of selling, there are some very important distinctions. As a Network Marketer, you would use a very different paradigm to achieve the same $1 million in sales.

Instead of full-time, professional salespeople with terrifying quotas, Network Marketing is based on satisfied customers, most of whom do not like to sell but are happy to tell others about the products they, themselves, use. These customers are not full-time or part-time employees. They are some-time, independent volunteers with no quotas and no protected territories. They "work" when they feel like it.

Network Marketing is not necessarily about personally selling a lot of product, although some Distributors do. It is about **using** and **recommending** the product and, IF you see and believe in the wealth building model of geometric progression, finding a lot of others to do the same.

The differences between **Salespeople** and **Network Marketing People** are:

Sales		Network Marketing
Full-time	**vs.**	Some Time
Salespeople	**vs.**	Customers
Employees	**vs.**	Volunteers
Quotas	**vs.**	Incentives
Protected Territories	**vs.**	No Territories

To Sell $1,000,000:

100 Salespeople each sell $10,000 = $1,000,000	**vs.**	10,000 Volunteers each sell $100 = $1,000,000

Network Marketing is simply a lot of people doing a little bit *each.*

CHAPTER 5

HOW IT WORKS

Nothing worthwhile really ever comes easily. Work, continuous work and hard work, is the only way you will accomplish results that last. Whatever you want in life, you must give up something to get it. The greater the value, the greater the sacrifice required of you.

There's a price to pay if you want to make things better, a price to pay for just leaving things as they are. The highway to success is a toll road. Everything has a price.

— UNKNOWN

How It Works

There Are Three Basic Activities Required To Create Your Own Four Year Career

1. Use ...

First, become your own best customer. USE all of your company's products in as many ways as possible discovering as many benefits and success stories as possible. Create your own best product story. You will want to be able to tell people exactly what this product did for you that made you want to use it forever and share it with others. The more powerful your own story, the more impact you will have in recommending the product to others—and most importantly you won't be "selling" it, you will just be telling your story.

2. Recommend ...

This is where most people think they have to sell the product. It's better to see yourself just recommending it, like you would a good movie or restaurant. You listen to the people around you ... listen to their problems. And when someone shares a problem your product can solve, just tell them your story. Let them decide if it is right for them. If you recommend a great Italian place and the person says, "I don't like Italian," then the conversation is probably over. If they say, "that place is too expensive," you just let it go as their opinion. You don't argue, right? Don't sell or argue with customers either. Just recommend it. If it is a fit, perfect. If not, let it go. This is how successful Network Marketers establish lots of customers over time and move lots of product without making a nuisance of themselves.

3. Invite ...

Inviting people is like recommending the product, only you are inviting them to "just take a look" at the income opportunity. The best way to do this is with a tool like a CD, DVD, brochure or website. Those who master inviting, eventually master The Four Year Career.

Again, this is not selling, convincing or arguing. People are either ready in their life right now to look at new options or they are not. Arguing with them about whether they have time, the money to get started or whether they are good at selling is a waste of time and energy. (Although it is fun to "let" someone "sell" you hard on why they can't sell.)

You may not have as great of an income story to tell your prospects as you do your product story. That is what your "upline" partners are for. Tell their stories. There are just a few keys to being an effective inviter:

1. Be convinced yourself ... in your product, your company and The Four Year Career. Your conviction should show up as enthusiasm, confidence, peace, patience, acceptance, love and leadership.
2. Be interesting. Not by what you say, what you drive, how you hype but by being interested ... interested in them. Ask curiosity questions and LISTEN. Make it all about them and they will be honored and become interested in you ... ergo interested in anything you are doing.
3. Mastery comes with practice ... 10,000 hours of practice which might convert to 5,000 conversations over Four Years. You are not in the game unless you are inviting new people to

look every day, every week. You are not in the game if you are just thinking about it, worrying about it, avoiding it, getting organized to do it or getting trained to do it perfectly. Two a day and 10 in play is the perfect plan. Invite two new people every day and follow up on the last 10 you invited until they say "Yes" or "No."

CHAPTER

6

Four Cornerstones of
The Four Year Career

The American Pioneers HAD to become successful entrepreneurs
… the Native Americans wouldn't hire them.

— Richard Bliss Brooke

Four Cornerstones of The Four Year Career

This Is What You Are Looking To Build As An Example of The Numbers:

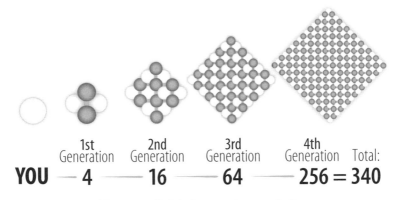

YOU	1st Generation	2nd Generation	3rd Generation	4th Generation	Total:
	4	16	64	256 = 340

You enroll 4 (who each enroll 4)

for 16 (who each enroll 4)

for 64 (who each enroll 4) for 256

Each of you uses and recommends just an average of $100 a month in products for $34,000 in monthly sales. Earning an average of 10% on each generation of sales for a Residual Income of $3,410 a month.

The Four Cornerstones of The Four Year Career:

1. People
2. Product Sales
3. Your Royalty Income
4. The Residual Asset Value

First let's talk about THE PEOPLE. Who are they? Where do they come from? Why do we need them? Let's understand HOW sales are produced in the Network Marketing model.

The First Cornerstone is People

Network Marketing is a lot of people doing a little bit each, as opposed to a traditional sales business model where a few people do a lot. In traditional sales, $1 million in sales might be achieved with 100 superstar sales reps, each with a $10,000 quota. In Network Marketing, you swap the numbers: 10,000 "anybody" volunteers each doing an average of $100 in sales. So how does one get 10,000 people, or even 1,000?

Two laws allow us to gather 1,000 people. The first was written by the creators for the Network Marketing concept who said, in essence: "Anyone can, and should sponsor others." This allows the second law: Geometric Progression.

This is How The Rich Get Richer and
The Poor Get Poorer

If you had $1 million today to invest at 10%:

- In 7 years, you would have $2 million.
- In 14 years, you would have $4 million.
- In 21 years, you would have $8 million.

With $8 million at 10% you would be earning $800,000 a year in interest alone. Eventually, whether it is at $800k a year or $2 million a year, you tire of spending it (on things that you do not appreciate).

In many "old money" families, this investment compounding has gone on for so many generations, they can't possibly spend all the interest income produced. They are on autopilot to just keep getting richer.

- Geometric Progression is to Network Marketing what compounding is to wealth building.
- Remember the comparison of Network Marketing to traditional sales? 100 people vs 1,000?
- The question is, how do you get 1,000 people to be "recommending for you?"
- The answer is, you don't. You just get a few ... like four, and lead them to do the same.

The path to gathering 1,000, 2,000 or 30,000 people to "sell for you" in Network Marketing is geometric progression. This is made possible by the Rule of Law in Network Marketing ... that everyone regardless of rank or time involved is encouraged to invite and enroll

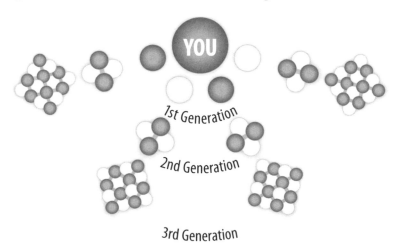

Note: No Network Marketer's organization looks exactly like this one. This is merely an illustration of a mathematical formula that shows the dynamic and potential available. There is no way to control how many, or how few, people any one Distributor will sponsor.

others. If you have been involved for one day you are encouraged to invite and enroll others. This is the same if you have been involved for 10 years and are earning $10,000 a month. Everyone enrolls new sales representatives. This creates the compounding impact.

You enroll four who each enroll four who each enroll four, etc. 1 – 4 – 16 – 64 – 256 – 1,024 and so on. And you only enrolled four.

It's Not Nearly As Easy As It Appears On Paper

This progression can quickly be overwhelming. But your role in Network Marketing is just to get the first four – not the whole bunch. Focus your attention on just the first four. And in actuality you may build in units of 2 or 3 … the same concept holds true.

The key to believing in getting 1,000 or 2,000 people on your team is to break the whole process down into a duplicatable bite size piece. And that piece is how many you (and just you) can get. The belief lies in a simple question you can ask yourself:

> *"If you really, really wanted to,* could you find four people, anywhere in North America, any occupation, any adult age, any education, to do this? Before you answer—let's define "do this."

It is defined as using the product, recommending it to other people and inviting others on a consistant basis to look at the opportunity … just to look.

So I ask you again. If you really, really wanted to, could you find four?

Most people would answer yes. The reason is, if they really "wanted to," anything like this is doable. Getting four people to make a fortune is not THAT hard to do.

If you answered YES … lock in on that YES; it is the key to believing you can get 10,000. Why? Because if you believe you will get four and they are four who are "doing it," then they also believe they will get four. If you are not sure … ask them. And what is usually the result of someone really, really wanting to do something—but more importantly—believing they will do it and being in action doing it?

You are probably "getting it" right now. This is how geometric progression will work for you. Just believing in your four and teaching and motivating them to do the same … one person each believing they will get four creates … You – 4 – 16 – 64 – 256 – 1,024 and so on.

The Second Cornerstone is Product Sales

Compared to the rest of the Four Year Career Cornerstones, people are the most important and most challenging aspect to understand, believe in and execute. Product Sales, however, are not. In a legitimate Network Marketing business, the brand representatives are very satisfied customers … one  could even say evangelical. They love the product. They love it so much they open their mind to becoming a Network Marketer and recommending it.

Some will ask after seeing all the geometric progression of recruiting ... "well if everyone is recruiting who will sell the product?" I like to let people think for a moment about what they just asked. The answer is Grant's Tomb obvious. *Everyone* is selling the product. And the more people we have selling it the more we sell. We just don't worry about how much any one representative sells.

The average Network Marketer might only personally use and sell $100–$300 a month. There will always be exceptions. There are people who sell thousands a month. But as long as the product is compelling, the sales reps will sell it ... or more accurately recommend it. Sales are simply created by the Distributors using and offering products. So if you have 2,000 representitives each averaging $200 a month in consumption and sales, your business generates $400,000 a month in sales.

The Third Cornerstone is Royalty Income

This is the easiest cornerstone to understand and believe. Every Network Marketing company has a compensation plan that pays you on most, if not all, of the many levels of representatives in your group. This is the percent of sales volume you will earn on each generation of brand representatives.

Each company is very creative to incentivize (yes, this is now a word) certain business building behaviors. The bottom line is you can expect to earn between 5 and 10% on the sales of your entire organization providing you qualify to earn at the deepest generations. This gives you Royalty Income. If your sales are $400,000 a month, you are earning between $20,000 and $40,000 a month.

The Fourth Cornerstone is The Residual Aspect of Your Income and The Asset Value

If you continue to use the theoretical model of four who sponsor four, etc., then at some point perhaps around year two or three, 256 people would fill your fourth level (or generation) of Distributors. This would result in a total of 340 people in your Network Marketing organization.

If each of those Distributors use and recommend just $200 of product per month, there would be 340 people selling a total of $68,000 worth of product monthly.

If you're paid an average royalty of 10% on that $68,000, your monthly check would be $6,800.

If you could count on it continuing long after you were building it then it is deemed residual and will have a corresponding asset value. $6,800 a month for example is worth about $1,200,000 at a 7% annualized return over the course of 10 years.

Examples of other income producing assets would be real estate, dividend producing stocks, patent and copyright royalties. All of these can be appraised for a value based on their income history and future income prospects.

Think about it. What is your home worth? If you own it, what could you rent it for? If you are renting, you already know. If your home is worth $250,000 you might rent it for $1,500 a month or a 7% annual return on the owner's investment.

Although you cannot sell a Distributorship for $1,200,000 that earns $6,800 a month (far too easy for one to build on their own), it is worth that to you as an asset.

So how do you know it will be residual?

The Answer ... Is In The Numbers

Look closely at the generations diagram that follows. Which generation earns you the most income? Obviously, it is the fourth generation, which has four times as many people in it as the third generation before it. In fact, more than 75% of your group's sales volume—and therefore, over 75% of your earnings—are from your fourth generation Distributors.

In this scenario, however, we are assuming your fourth generation people are just getting started in the business. Hopefully, they are inviting everyone to have a look, but they have not yet sponsored anyone themselves, so we do not show a fifth generation.

Sooner or later this may change, and when each fourth generation Distributor gets their four, you would have added 1,024 new

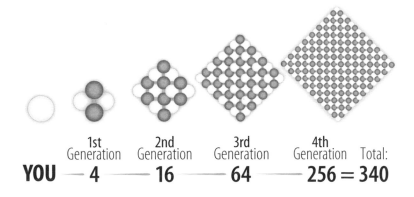

Distributors to your fifth generation. At $100 per Distributor in sales, and with a 10% royalty, that translates into an additional $102,400 in sales and an additional $10,240 in monthly earnings for you.

THIS ONE PIECE OF THE PUZZLE PULLS IT ALL TOGETHER.

WHEN YOU UNDERSTAND THIS PIECE, YOU ARE LIKELY TO "GET IT" AND START TO UNDERSTAND THE POSSIBILITIES OF THE FOUR YEAR CAREER.

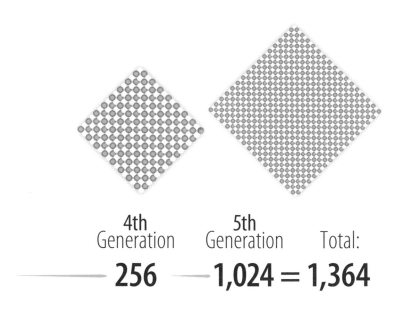

4th Generation	5th Generation	Total:
256	**1,024**	**= 1,364**

Everyone we have shown thus far in this hypothetical plan is what we call a Sales Leader. We have shown that each one gets four. In order to get four to actually "do this" or be a Sales Leader, each Sales Leader will have enrolled many more than just four. Your first four are not likely to be "the four." Each Sales Leader will likely enroll 20–100 people in order to get their own four Sales Leaders. The point is that in *The Four Year Career* we only show Sales Leaders … the best of the best. The best product promoters, the best trainers, the best motivators and the best enrollers. So when I say your 4th generation has YET to enroll anyone, what I mean is given that they are Sales Leaders … they will enroll four or more.

So calculate what happens to your "residual" income when they each get their own four … it grows by 400%. The definition of Residual Income is that it just remains static … that it never grows at all.

So what about all the non Sales Leaders? What about the majority of new Distributors who did not end up "doing it." Some quit and never continue even using the product. Some give up on the income opportunity but remain loyal customers. Some sell a little and some even sponsor a few people here and there. But they are not Sales Leaders and NONE of them are shown in this plan. If you add them back in …

One last way to look at the possibility of Residual Income is to look at the longevity of some of the biggest companies in the industry. Many are 25–50 years in the business and growing. That could only happen if this concept worked.

What it means is, if you ever have to (or choose to) stop building your Network Marketing business, the cash should keep on coming!

CHAPTER

7

THE ASSET VALUE

If we don't change our direction we're
likely to end up where we're headed.

— CHINESE PROVERB

THE ASSET VALUE

A reasonably capable person in the right Network Marketing company can create a monthly Residual Royalty Income of $2,500 within a couple of years of part-time effort, a million-dollar Distributorship within three to four years, and benefits can be doubled by using the extra income that a Network Marketing business generates to fuel an investment portfolio. How would it feel to be able to invest $5,000 into your future every month for the next 10 years?

As described in previous chapters, examples of other income producing assets would be real estate, dividend producing stocks, patent and copyright royalties. All of these can be appraised for a value based on their income history and future income prospects.

Let's look at asset value of residual income through Network Marketing.

	1st Generation	2nd Generation	3rd Generation	4th Generation	Total:
YOU —	**4** —	**16** —	**64** —	**256** =	**340**

$200 sales each x 340 people = $68,000

If each person has $200 in sales, that's 340 people earning a total sales of $68,000. You could earn an average of 10%[*] on all of it per month:

$68,000 x 10%[*] = $6,800 a month = $1,200,000 Asset Value

$6,800 a month for example is worth about $1,200,000 at a 7% annualized return over the course of 10 years.

[*]Industry average.

Build your network right and its sales and your income should flow long after you have anything to do with actively managing or growing it. That does not mean you ignore it or fail to nurture it. When we build or buy something that produces income without working it daily, it becomes an asset worth money in proportion to the income it produces.

Although you cannot sell a Distributorship for $1,200,000 that earns $6,800 a month (far too easy for one to build on their own), it nonetheless is worth that to you as an asset.

In pursuing financial security or more from life, people tend to pursue real estate investments or stocks (which require money to invest). These investments require time to produce enough income to provide security. Imagine or calculate how long, and at what rate of investment, it would require to amass $1 million in real estate. Not your residence, but rental real estate. It could easily take a lifetime of sacrifice, risk and management. And $1 million in real estate might earn you $5,000 a month.

Compare that to investing $1,000 once and only 10-20 hours a week for four to five years to earn the same residual income with an asset value of $1,200,000. Which is more appealing and more achievable to you? Yeah, us too.

Now take it a step further and think about a powerful Three Prong Approach. You are building a million dollar residual income asset in Network Marketing while at the same time investing $1,000 a month, then $2,000, $3,000 and ultimately $5,000 a month in real estate, stocks, bonds, etc. Ten years of this and you could be a multi-millionaire with three sources of residual income.

CHAPTER **8**

MOMENTUM

Insanity: Doing the same thing over and over again
and expecting different results.

— ALBERT EINSTEIN

Momentum

Launching a Network Marketing sales group is much like pushing a car over a very slight hill. Imagine that you ran out of gas as you were driving up a hill. At the top of the hill the road becomes flat for some period of time and then slightly descends to the bottom of the hill where there is a gas station. Your mission is to get out of the car, get it rolling up the slight hill, to the top, keep it going on the flat section until you crest the hill. Then you hop in and ride it to riches.

This is the same. In the beginning, you will exert the most amount of effort promoting the product and enrolling new people for the least amount of return. Once you get things rolling it will take less effort to keep them rolling but you must still keep pushing to keep it going. Once you hit "momentum" you just hop in and ride the wave.

Momentum happens at different times in different companies. You will know it when you are in it. You will not be able to keep up with the help requests people have for you and your group will be on fire.

Think of it like starting out pushing a Smart Car up the hill, having it turn into a Cadillac at the top and a Ferrari at the downhill crest.

It is the low return on effort in the beginning that leads most people to give up. They do not have the Vision and Belief in the payoffs on the other side.

Launching Your Business (1-2 years)

Maximum Effort For Least Results

You Have Got The Ball Rolling But. . . (2-4 years)

Less Effort But You Still Cannot Let Off

Critical Mass Your Income Becomes Residual

Get In And Ride The Wave

Another way to look at the growth of your group is to look at the Penny a Day chart. If it took a lot of effort to double that penny, given the return on investment of effort, most people would quit. Even half way through the month it is only worth $163.84! Yet if you understand the power of geometric progression and compounding then you KNOW if you keep doubling it, that little penny is worth over $5 million at the end of the month.

Day 1	$0.01	Day 16	$327.68
Day 2	$0.02	Day 17	$655.36
Day 3	$0.04	Day 18	$1,310.72
Day 4	$0.08	Day 19	$2,621.44
Day 5	$0.16	Day 20	$5,242.88
Day 6	$0.32	Day 21	$10,485.76
Day 7	$0.64	Day 22	$20,971.52
Day 8	$1.28	Day 23	$41,943.04
Day 9	$2.56	Day 24	$83,886.08
Day 10	$5.12	Day 25	$167,772.16
Day 11	$10.24	Day 26	$335,544.32
Day 12	$20.48	Day 27	$671,088.64
Day 13	$40.96	Day 28	$1,342,177.28
Day 14	$81.92	Day 29	$2,684,354.56
Day 15	$163.84	Day 30	$5,368,709.12

After 30 days, 1 penny becomes over 5 million dollars!

CHAPTER 9

THE RENAISSANCE OF THE FAMILY & COMMUNITY

It's what you learn after you know it all that really counts.

— COACH JOHN WOODEN

THE RENAISSANCE OF THE FAMILY & COMMUNITY

Yes, it is true that building a sales organization of on-fire volunteers is still a challenge. However, it is being done, and in a powerful way. The biggest challenge is in erasing people's negative beliefs and biases about the Network Marketing concept and replacing them with what those of us who have already done it know to be true. And, it's coming ... one day soon, world consciousness will shift and most people—yes, most everyone—will in some way be a part of this dynamic, wealth-building industry.

Opportunity appreciation is not the only factor fueling the future of Network Marketing. It is also fueled by people's basic need to connect with others, to be a part of something bigger than themselves, and to have a sense of community.

Most of us know all too well that the family has disintegrated in many segments of our country. Since family is the foundation of neighborhoods and communities, they too have been compromised. Most of the industrialized world is deeply entrenched in the rat race—parents with full-time careers, day care, career advancement, soccer, music lessons, phones, faxes, e-mail, Internet, pagers, cell phones and Blackberry/iPhone mania—payments, payments and more payments. Some of us are winning the race, but it has been said, "We are still rats!"

Today, people are longing for a return to a real, safe, relaxed time of freedom and soulful connection with others. People want to play together, pray together, get to really know each other, and most importantly, to be known by others.

We want to improve ourselves, to have more pride in ourselves, to love and respect ourselves. We are hungry for guidance and support that will help us grow to be more powerful, more generous and more self-assured. Anyone who has come full circle can tell you that there are things that bring true happiness. Happiness is "being" home.

Achieving financial success and status are wonderful, especially if the alternative is being financially strapped to a life of despair. I think we'd all be better off rich, but money is relative—the more you have, the more you think you need.

Or, as it has been said, "Money is relative. The more you have, the more **relatives** you have." There is a point, however, where we must have the wisdom to know when enough is enough.

This return to basic human values in business is a subtle, yet powerful force driving the Network Marketing industry. By its very nature, Network Marketing is a people-intensive business. If you pursue it, you will have people—thousands of them—supercharged into your life. You will have your group, your upline, your local area group, and your entire company as extended family and community groups.

These are the qualities that will endear you to your family and to the community you create:

Patience	Honesty	Forthrightness
Generosity	Integrity	Leadership
Open-mindedness	Authenticity	Love
Cooperation	Courage	Listening

Network Marketing may offer the most dynamic environment within which we can develop our spirituality, and manage our humanity at the same time. It's a journey most people find exhilarating.

10

WHAT TO LOOK FOR IN A NETWORK MARKETING COMPANY

A building has integrity just like a man. And just as seldom.

— AYN RAND

What To Look For In A Network Marketing Company

1. Product

You must find a product or service you absolutely love:

- Something you would buy forever, regardless of whether or not you are a Distributor.
- Something you can recommend to others without reservation.

If you have to *try* to feel this way about the product, let it go. It will not work for you long term. Less important (but still vital) is that the product or service is consumable, which means that the customer is required to regularly buy more.

Look at the list of billion dollar companies and look at what kinds of products they sell. Ask yourself ... will this product really be relevant 25 years from now? Will it be in demand? Will it still be able to be competitively priced? Technology and service products are challenged here. They need to be constantly reinvented to stay relevant and competitive. Pick your product line with an eye on the long term. How long term? How long do you want to get paid? I prefer forever.

2. The Company

You must be proud of and trust the company: your "mothership" and its leaders. They are your partners in product development, legal and financial issues, human resources, customer service, product development, order fulfillment, data processing, international expansion, public relations, ethics and culture. They are crucial to your long-term success.

Imagine working hard for two or three years to build a solid Network Marketing group, then having the company go out of business or embarrass you and your group so badly that everyone wants to quit.

3. Your Upline

These are the people above you in your line of sponsorship. They will be partnering with you, training you and supporting you. You will be spending countless hours with them. They will be in your home, and you in theirs. You may be earning them a lot of money. You must at least like them. Preferably you will love, honor and respect them.

Look for people who are dedicated, loyal, focused, positive, committed, generous and successful. Hook your wagon onto a rising Network Marketing star and you will increase your probability of success immensely. And most importantly, once you choose your sponsor and upline, listen to them. Follow their lead. Get trained by them. Be coachable. They can only be successful if you are successful.

Choose Your Company Wisely

You're encouraged to use this book as the beginning of your Network Marketing education. Be a student. Do your homework. Start by talking frankly with whomever had the vision and courage to give you this book.

If you can, find the right product, company and people for you. If you can't, keep looking. Don't settle by copping out or by looking for reasons why it won't work. Instead, look with the intention of finding the right match—no matter how long it takes or what it requires of you.

When you find a company to call home, build your empire. Don't be deterred by challenges and setbacks; even dumb mistakes your "home" may make. Stick with them through thick and thin. Your life and the lives of thousands may be enriched. The world is waiting ...

If you have questions about a company, the Direct Selling Association (DSA) in Washington, D.C., is the professional association that represents and sets high standards for the Network Marketing industry. The DSA has been in existence for over 100 years. You may visit their website at DSA.org.

SUCCESS STORIES

The following stories feature people who perhaps may be much like you. Certainly in their beginning they didn't understand or necessarily believe in the promise of Network Marketing. And as you will read most were not instant successes. Many of them have the same story as most people who get involved during their first few months or even years ... "This doesn't work!"

Yet if you can reflect on the examples of duplication, compounding and the car over the hill, it might help you make sense of these massive success stories. This is a much bigger opportunity than most people believe. And that is The Promise of Network Marketing ... that it's just an opportunity. What you do with it is up to you.

JANINE AVILA

Janine Avila rose to No. 1 Recruiter among more than a half million Tupperware managers worldwide.

Janine Avila is filled with a contagious spirit and boundless energy that nurtures and empowers others. That is what makes her a highly respected international speaker, author, trainer and coach. Over the past 25 years, she has become a well-known leader in the Network Marketing industry, both as a Distributor and at the corporate level.

Her introduction to Network Marketing came almost out of necessity. A single mother of seven, five biological and two adopted, Janine searched for a way to create financial security—without missing out on her childrens' lives.

As a result, she developed simple and effective systems for team building and time management, which she credits for her meteoric rise to the top recruiter spot among more than 500,000 Tupperware managers around the world.

After building an empire with Tupperware, the networking trailblazer went on to build successful organizations with several other companies. Janine's ability to develop and motivate Distributors makes her highly sought after throughout the industry. She has held positions as Senior Vice President of Sales and Marketing and Vice President of Training for two prominent Network Marketing companies. Janine's passion for training others to create controlled, predictable incomes has never wavered. The philosophy on which she built her success is: "Build the people and the people will build the business."

Traveling the world, Janine shares the stage with legends such as Les Brown, Jim Rohn, Richard Brooke, Brian Tracy, the late John Kalench, Dan McCormick, Jerry Clark and other personal development and Network Marketing experts.

In her private life, Janine has overcome seemingly impossible obstacles, such as a stroke that robbed her of her ability to speak. She worked tirelessly to teach herself to speak again by listening to her own voice on countless training programs she had previously recorded. Having regained her speech—and with a renewed level of enthusiasm—she delivered a memorable speech at the Direct Selling Association leadership event in 2007.

"It's not what happens in your life—it's how you respond to it. You're always going to have problems. It's like Rocky Balboa; when you get knocked down you have to climb back up the ropes and keep on fighting." It's a strong message for Network Marketers, says Janine, who continues to actively build her business and show others what's possible.

"It's not what happens in your life – it's how you respond to it."

Janine lives in Visalia, California. Her children are grown and she enjoys spending time with her grandchildren and her freedom.

Visit JanineAvila.com

ANN FEINSTEIN

Ann Feinstein was named one of the Top 100 Direct Selling Mentors and is a featured speaker at global Network Marketing events.

Growing up in Pennsylvania, Ann Feinstein's parents told her to go to college, get a good education and she would be secure. Following that advice, she graduated and became a high school English teacher and Drama Coach.

Jumping on an opportunity to move to NYC, Ann made a transition into the business world as Director of Research for a leading Park Avenue consulting firm. It was there that her first entrepreneurial mentor told her, "Ann, the only security you will ever have in life is what you create for yourself!"

Reflecting back, that was a game changing moment for her in her early 30's, sitting in a cubicle, feeling like a prisoner of that 40-story office building, contemplating what her next career step should be to break free.

Along the way, she met the love of her life, David, a NYC business manager in the entertainment industry. Seeing the business world through David's entrepreneurial eyes, Ann became even more determined to break free from her weekly 70-hour-plus corporate bondage.

Every weekend Ann and David took refuge at their New Jersey horse farm, dreading the drive back through the Lincoln Tunnel each Monday.

They were determined to find a serious business they could work together to free them from their corporate and small business grind, and utilize their unique talents.

While attending a personal development course in 1987, they were introduced to Network Marketing by a new friend they made there, and knew they had found their perfect storm of opportunity.

With David's support, Ann began developing their business part-time in the evenings and weekends, while continuing her full-time job. During that time, David saw the freedom Ann was enjoying and decided to sell his practice and joined Ann full-time. That partnership has produced extraordinary results.

Over the next 18 years, their organization expanded into 13 countries with over 100,000 team members, even before the Internet. That experience prepared them for their next opportunity of building a multi-million dollar team in more than 40 countries.

Ann and David are Executive Diamond Directors, serving on their company's Leadership Advisory Council. Ann was named one of the Top 100 Direct Selling Mentors and is a featured speaker at global Network Marketing events, while David has become a recognized contributor to many Network Marketing publications. Their company honored the Feinsteins with the prestigious "Global Ambassador" and "Inspiration of the Year" awards.

Having the time of their lives traveling the world together, Ann and David recently moved back home to Bucks County, Pennsylvania just when their family needed them. Now that's REAL FREEDOM!

Their organization expanded into 13 countries with over 100,000 team members, even before the Internet.

Visit AnnFeinstein.com

JORDAN ADLER

Jordan Adler, drawn to entrepreneurial-type opportunities, earns seven figures a year and donates 100% of his book profits to charity.

Jordan was introduced to the Network Marketing profession back in the 80's when he picked up a book on the subject for 25 cents at a garage sale. He was intrigued by the idea of passive residual income. Although he grew up in a working class neighborhood, he was always drawn to entrepreneurial type opportunities.

Jordan's father preached the value of a college degree and getting a good job, but Jordan was drawn to business ideas that could someday make him a fortune.

Although he worked lots of different jobs to pay his bills, he started answering classified ads offering the promise of financial freedom. He joined and quit 11 companies in his first 10 years in the profession. Yet, he was a sponge for learning the business of Network Marketing. He attended many seminars and read hundreds of books. But he never sponsored a single person and never received a check for his first 10 years in Network Marketing.

Then, Jordan joined his 12th Network Marketing company in 1992 and went on to make over $8 million. He learned that one's success has everything to do with one's focus, determination, attitude and willingness to take productive action. Once he realized that he wouldn't find success outside of himself, everything changed. He adopted the philosophy of 'Don't quit on a bad day.'

He sponsors an average of one person per week and has grown his team to about 60,000 people. He has earned seven figures a year in his current company for the past four consecutive years.

Jordan loves Network Marketing because it offers a chance for anyone to create positive financial growth without any formal experience and little to no capital risk. And he believes, "Success in Network Marketing is directly related to the degree in which one can give to others without the expectation of getting something in return."

"Don't quit on a bad day."

Jordan is the author of the best-selling book *Beach Money: Creating Your Dream Life Through Network Marketing.* He is proud of the fact that 100% of the profits from the book go to charity.

Visit Beachmoney.com

MARGIE ALIPRANDI

Margie Aliprandi, from humble beginnings, overcame all odds and is now a world renowned Network Marketing success.

Twenty years ago, Margie Aliprandi was a junior high music teacher, a single mom with three little children and had no capital. She had dreams of saving her home and providing a better life for her children, but her salary just wouldn't cut it. She was looking for something else when she found a product and company she fell in love with. She found herself excited and at a crossroads. Margie threw caution to the wind, canceled her teaching contract and decided to tackle Network Marketing full-time.

Fast forward and you'll find Margie as an energetic international speaker, author and trainer. Within one year of starting her business in Network Marketing she had a five-figure monthly income, and after three years she was at millionaire status.

How did she do it? Perseverance. No matter what it took, she was willing to do it. Her "why" was her children's welfare, and it was so powerful that she looked right past any obstacles and focused on their future.

Today, Margie has four grown children who have experienced the world together, and their idea of family has expanded to include people throughout the world. They have watched their mom mentor people internationally. She says, "My greatest role today is cheerleading people for their large and small successes and helping them feel 'seen' for where they are. My children's lives are richer for the experiences and what they've witnessed in a mother who had so many doubts, yet consistently rose above them—because, ultimately, that's what I did. When I look at them now, I see the people who they have become in large part because I was an entrepreneurial parent. Perhaps I was a better mom because I was living my dream and in the process enabled them to expand theirs too."

"Perseverance is the ultimate habit in networking."

"For some, it happens right away, for most, it takes dedication. Keep sowing seeds. You cannot sow only two seeds and expect a big harvest. It's the 80/20 rule so plant seeds every day if you want your business to explode."

Visit MargieAliprandi.com

NICK SARNICOLA

Nick Sarnicola made his first million by age 25 and his team enrolled 100,000 new customers and produced $20 million a month in sales.

Nick grew up in Grand Rapids, Michigan in an extremely blue collar, middle class family. His grandparents put 120 years into the same factory among the four of them, spawning three generations of would-be factory workers. At a very early age he knew he wouldn't be one of them. Unaware of entrepreneurship, he figured baseball would be his way out. Thankfully at the age of 18, he was recruited into Network Marketing while working part-time at the local mall.

He started in Network Marketing with zero business or sales experience other than selling clothes. He immediately fell deeply in love with the industry. Even though he made no money, something intuitively was screaming that he was in the right place doing the right thing ...

It took him four years to make a six figure a year income. Not bad for a 22 year old community college dropout.

With his initial success and some fortuitous adversity, Nick partnered with Blake Mallen and Ryan Blair and they founded their own Network Marketing company. Nick thought his role would be a Vice President with a big corner office. But, that was not to be. He did something bold, something virtually unheard of.

He did about the most illogical thing someone could do in his position. He resigned at age 31 as the CSO to sign back up in his own company as a Distributor. He went from having guaranteed income, budgets, staff, and a corner office in Beverly Hills to having no income, no budgets, and no staff. But what he did have was a shot to prove to his leaders as a trench general that their model would work.

Twenty-four months later, Nick had led his sales team in enrolling up to 100,000 new customers a month and producing $20 million dollars a month in sales. (Yes, you read that right. Think 'Ferrari' over the hill.)

With all possible odds against them, their team and their company rose to the top, putting his total earnings from Network Marketing at over $10 million dollars over 14 years. It has been a dream come true from every sense of the term.

- It's hard work, but not compared to digging ditches.
- You can make money doing anything; do this because you love people.
- Sell out. Don't half-ass it. No "one foot in, one foot out."
- Be committed to continual personal growth.
- Leaders make the long-term sustainable money. Learn to lead.
- Sell your way out of your problems. Keep recruiting.
- Build it with someone you love.
- Keep belief and faith at all times.
- Find the champion within you.

Visit NickSarnicola.com

ONYX COALE

Onyx Coale is one of the highest paid women in the Direct Selling Industry. Her estimated life time earnings are $14+ million in 6 years. She prides herself on creating leaders and changing lives one person at a time.

Network Marketing was introduced to Onyx for the first time 6 years ago. Her babysitter's parents were the ones to introduce her to the profession, and are still her sponsors today. She said "NO" many times before she finally went to their house and listened to a presentation. Onyx says, "Once I saw those circles being drawn, tasted the product, and I saw the power of the compensation plan, I knew it was a serious business opportunity."

Onyx has only been with one Network Marketing company. She is a single mom who has built a personal organization of over 340,000 Distributors. She is a Royal Black Diamond with her company (only 12 people company-wide have reached that rank) and has helped over

50 people earn more than a million dollars in Network Marketing.

If you want to build a residual income, Onyx says that you need to find a company that will allow you to create a long-term plan. She prefers a company with an auto ship program. Why? Because it lets you create a residual income stream (that means you get paid over and over for the work you did one time). Her goal is to teach others to look for a company whose structure is set up with a consumable product that people need. Auto ship will send them their product monthly, so everyone continues to make money even though they only sold the product one time. As Onyx would say, "Sweeeeet!!!"

Onyx often tells the story of how it took her five years to put herself through college costing her thousands of dollars. She did this, like many others, hoping to get a $60,000 a year job. She later learned that if you spend a mere four years in Network Marketing, the odds are that you are going to earn a lot more than $60,000 per year without taking loans to do so! And let's face it, Network Marketing is a whole lot easier than college and SO much more fun.

She will be the first to tell you that she came to this industry kicking and screaming. While she has been able to build, support, and grow a very large business, Onyx makes sure to reiterate that it doesn't happen overnight. Like everyone, she has had to develop herself so that she could continue to build her business mind and connect with new and different people. Though she is dyslexic, Onyx has learned how to work through it and has read thousands of books. She continues to read avidly and attend every seminar she thinks could help her reach her dream of helping others.

Onyx strives to share the information she has learned, which has allowed her to help create many leaders. Her style of leadership is called "situational leadership." She meets people where they're at and helps them discover what they need to learn about themselves so that they can grow both personally and professionally. She doesn't duplicate, she creates. This allows each individual to build upon their strengths and accomplish their own goals. "I believe that all people are different, especially when you take your business internationally."

One lesson that Onyx feels is imperative for everyone is the importance of choices. How you choose to deal with adversity can actually propel your success to new heights. A decisive moment in her Network Marketing career was when Onyx did not reach her goal date for a car incentive. "I had a choice; pick a new date and keep working or quit. I kept going. The day I helped another woman earn her own free Mercedes—WOW. I knew I was living my life's purpose."

Equally important is choosing how to use your time. Onyx doesn't believe in balance. Instead, she chooses to be fully present and focused on what she is doing. Onyx explains, "My average day looks very different depending on whether I'm home or traveling for my teams. If I am home, I make the kids breakfast and take them to school. While they are at school, I work with my groups on the phone or on Skype. I pick my kids up from school and I make sure I am fully present for them. If I am traveling with my teams, I am meeting people, leading meetings, taking calls, etc. I am focused on growing the business."

"Sure I now have time freedom, and financial freedom, but I have so much more," Onyx says. "I have learned MANY things about myself, and I get to live my life's purpose—helping others. I think few people in the world get the pleasure of living their life's purpose. Beyond having a ball and helping others, my business keeps growing and I have been honored to help create many new Network Marketing millionaires."

"The more you learn, the more you earn."

Pursuing her mission to help others, Onyx continues to promote the Network Marketing profession as a path to a more prosperous, well-rounded lifestyle. This begins with continuing to make time to invite new recruits into her business and give presentations. Her approach has helped her organization grow to include members in North America, Europe, Australia, New Zealand and Southeast Asia.

"My best tip for ANYONE in this business is to master the skill of 'inviting.' This is the single MOST important activity in the Network Marketing business. When you master this skill, NO one will be able to stop your business from exploding!!!"

Visit OnyxCoale.com

TODD FALCONE

Todd Falcone, since 1990 has built five different successful Network Marketing organizations and consistently earns in the six figures.

No matter how successful Todd Falcone has become, he still considers himself just an average guy. He grew up in a very middle-class family with no kind of entrepreneurial upbringing whatsoever.

His stepfather was not wealthy, but comfortably successful. Todd had an opportunity to see a direct comparison between broke and comfortable, and comfortable seemed a lot more appealing to him.

Todd ended up going to college. He surfed every day and skipped class often, but still wanted to be successful in his life. As he was graduating, he got a call from someone he thought was recruiting him ... into a job. (Todd was actually being recruited into the Network Marketing business!)

In that first experience Todd was hooked. He saw freedom and no boss, and THAT sounded good to him. The choice was easy. He gave them $1,000, and started his Network Marketing career.

The first two years were a dismal failure from the standpoint of generating any money. Most people quit when they don't make anything ... but Todd FELT that this was something he could make work, in spite of dismal results. He was simply willing to stay put and stay focused. His success is a result of staying put and not quitting, coupled with an ongoing focus on getting better at what we do in this business.

Fast forward: Todd has been in the profession of Network Marketing for over 22 years. He has built five different companies during those 22 years to what most people would consider the "top" of their compensation plans. He has had groups in excess of 18,000 people, and has been one of the most consistent earners year in, year out for nearly two decades.

Todd has been happily jobless for a very LONG time and considers himself totally unemployable at this point in his life, even though his earnings have consistently averaged in the multiple six-figures.

Todd got involved in Network Marketing because he saw FREEDOM. He didn't do it because he saw himself owning a private jet or a Rolls Royce, but simply because he wanted to do whatever he wanted, when he felt like it. The most important aspect is being able to live his life on his terms and not someone else's. Network Marketing has also allowed him to travel and spend time with his kids.

"You're probably going to have to work hard no matter what you do or where you work, so you might as well do it someplace where the reward of you working hard actually pays off."

Network Marketing provides average people the opportunity to achieve greatness. "Greatness is in all of us, and Network Marketing provides a vehicle for that greatness to grow." Todd is in for life.

Visit ToddFalcone.com

DANA COLLINS

Dana Collins catapulted herself into success with sales of over $6 million a month.

Immediately upon graduating from high school, Dana moved to NYC to attend the Fashion Institute of Technology (FIT). Through FIT, she was able to get recommended for an internship with a prominent designer. Her life was unfolding exactly as she had envisioned.

With this "dream job" came the dream wardrobe and shoes (of course), celebrities, fashion shows, travel and everything that looked exciting from the outside. In order to keep this "coveted job," she worked twelve hours a day on top of school. She had everything but a life.

Dana decided to pursue her dream job in her hometown of Baltimore, Maryland. She thought with her experience in the "Big Apple," opening her own boutique would be a no brainer.

But Dana soon found out that understanding fashion was only one part of owning a boutique.

Regrouping, she decided to go to work in the corporate world with a Fortune 500 company. One day, her boss called her into his office. Because she brought a new work ethic into a failing branch and taught others her success formula, the branch went from last to first in the company. She thought her boss was going to give her a promotion. Instead he said, "Privately, I will give you all the credit. Publicly, I am giving it to your male counterpart because I don't like to work with women." To say the least, she was in shock. How could this happen?

Finally, Dana got a job offer she was actually interested in: Network Marketing. She met her sponsor at a product trade show, and learned about the opportunity by being asked if she had ever thought about owning her own business. Dana laughed and put her hand up so fast she gave her sponsor whiplash. Even though she wasn't interested in starting another business, Dana listened to everything her sponsor said.

She knew that the woman she had met who introduced her to Network Marketing had the life she wanted and she loved the products.

One of the skills necessary to learn was to not attach herself to the outcome of any presentation. Once she really understood it was her job to tell the story of the company, the product, and the profession, and it wasn't her job to convince or sell anyone to join her, her business flourished. Within a few years she saw her volume grow close to $6 million each month with hundreds of leaders building alongside her.

"I am working with the best people I know. We help each other to become better; working toward reaching more of our potential. We give others the hope that they too can have both a dream job and a dream life."

What didn't look like a dream job has turned out to be more rewarding than she could have hoped for or imagined.

Visit Explorersclub.myarbonne.com

DONNA JOHNSON

Donna Johnson went from being a single mom with no college education to becoming a highly successful Executive National Vice President.

Donna grew up being a typical 'blue collar' Midwestern girl without a college education. She married young and subsequently found herself divorced with three small children at the age of 29. Then, she met the founder and product developer of a new marketing company. She fell in love with the incredible products and opportunity. She thought to herself, "It's too good to be true. What's the catch?" After some soul searching, and using the products, Donna knew it would be both good and true for her.

Donna started out just like any other representative, sharing the products she loved and the income opportunity she had grown to respect. Most of all Donna sold people ... people she met along the way to their own dreams. Dreams many of them had given up on.

These pages cannot do justice to the stories Donna can tell about the successes and the challenges. Suffice it to say, today her sales organization produces hundreds of millions a year with over 1 million sales representatives and over 1,000 of them driving white Mercedes Benz cars of their choice.

So what keeps Donna going? "This incredible gift that we keep on giving each and every day when we meet a new person. I call it '3-D Success ...' we all know many people who make a great income, but do they have the time to enjoy it? '3-D Success' means:

- Knowing what you do makes a difference
- Creating balance in your life
- Financial peace

Donna's Success Strategy: "Soar on your spirit wings!"

Believe in yourself, plug into the system and create your 'In for Life' story. Watch yourself talk. Talk and act like a top VP. Create excitement, passion, integrity and unity within your team. People want to follow someone who knows where they're going. If they know you, like you and trust you, you'll go far. We have a strong spirit of intent, derived from the Joni Erickson-Tada song, "Spirit Wings," which encourages us to love ourselves above all of the earthly things. So continue to be all that you can be, spread your wings, and soar on your Spirit Wings!"

Visit Donna.myarbonne.com

RANDY GAGE

Randy Gage's sales organization spans 65 countries and numbers more than 200,000 team members. He consistently earns over $1 million a year and growing, and has a fractional ownership in a moped which he subleases to Richard Brooke.

Randy Gage came from a small family; a single mother who raised three kids by herself, back in the day knocking on doors selling Avon products. And Randy really does mean his mom went out and knocked on doors, literally.

Randy's mother worked very hard and loved them all, and did her best to set a good example. She had character and a strong work ethic. They were poor. That presented challenges. And Randy never knew his father, but as he says, "My mother raised us good."

As for school ... Randy hated it.

He didn't fit in at all. He was pathologically shy and very insecure. He became a teenage alcoholic and drug addict. He skipped school, got suspended a lot, and finally was expelled before he was 16.

His first job was a dishwasher at a restaurant working for minimum wage. It was the only job he could get. He worked his way up to cook, waiter, host, and finally to a manager trainee, then assistant manager and eventually he made restaurant manager. "Which," he says, "is every dishwasher's dream."

Of course when he became the manager Randy realized that it wasn't the American dream—it was the American nightmare. He was working more hours and making less money than he made as a waiter.

Obviously, he thought, the secret is to own your own restaurant. Be your own boss. So, Randy and his assistant manager scraped together some money and leased a restaurant. That was "an unmitigated disaster." They ended up giving it back to the guy who had leased it to them and Randy went back in the business of managing.

Fortunately, along the way Randy had discovered Network Marketing and he made a little bit of money with it. He was working 14-15 hours a day in the restaurant, which left little time to do anything else, but he pursued both paths.

His first big check from Network Marketing was $11,000. That, plus some money he'd saved up, was enough to take on a new partner and try again with another restaurant. Sadly, this restaurant failed too.

As Randy says, "I was a slow learner."

Randy was 30 years old. No house, no car, no job, no money in the bank, no credit cards, and he was $55,000 in debt, which seemed like millions to him at the time. He was borrowing money from friends, selling the furniture…

That's when Randy told himself, "You know, I'm never going to pay off this debt in the restaurant business. If I do, it'll take me till I'm 60. I've got to get back into Network Marketing."

Randy started to make his way back and he's never looked back. He's made millions in Network Marketing.

"I grew up poor and I hated it," Randy says. "I was running away from being poor as much as I was running towards being rich, but they both were motivating me. The idea of leverage, being able to bring some people in, teach them, train them, and get a residual override on their productivity was really sexy. I got that one right away."

But Randy didn't get the business right away. It took about five years of losing money, going to events, buying tools, and negative cash flow that caused him to really do some critical thinking. "Okay, I've done a bunch of different companies, had different sponsors, different product lines and different compensation plans, and none of them have worked. So obviously, this is either a total fabrication that they made up to get my money or it's on me."

The point was, that in all of those companies there were people who were successful. There were people who were making money and they had the same product line and the same compensation plan and the same everything that Randy did, and yet they went out and created success.

He realized, "it's not on the business, it's not on the company; it's on me."

So, Randy made changes.

Once Randy took responsibility for his own success and failures, and committed himself to find a way for his company to work for him, everything changed. He discovered ways of building his group that were fun for him and ways that others in his group could duplicate … "This business is all about duplication."

"I've been able to mentor people who were living on welfare, raising their kids in the basement of a friend's house, who now make $30,000 a month. And it isn't the money really. The money's great, don't get me wrong, but I'm most excited for these people because it's the dignity it gives them, it's the belief it gives them."

"That's significant and that's what makes our business so amazing," Randy says.

"Network Marketing gives us an opportunity to create a legacy in very powerful and profound ways that you don't get to do in most other businesses. And that's really, really special."

"I believe in my work, because I believe in you."

Visit RandyGage.com

SUCCESS STORIES

The Success Stories in this issue are a sample of people I know who have made it big in Network Marketing and did it in an ethical and responsible manner in companies of the same character. Only one of them is in my own Network Marketing company.

If you would like to distribute a custom version of this book with just success stories of leaders in your company or organization, contact info@BlissBusiness.com

THANK YOU

Thank you for reading this book. We trust that you know a little more about the challenges and possibilities of the opportunity. And we trust that you can hear the voice inside you that tells you to resonate with these people and these ideas.

Anyone can be a successful brand representative of a product they love. And Network Marketing is full of unique, exclusive, powerful products. It has to be. It relies on the recommendations of its best customers for the product sales.

But this book is about something else. It is about the opportunity for you to see the possibilities of building a fortress of financial security around you and your family. Building your own little or big empire. Even $1,000 a month for the next 20 years invested wisely will set you up forever. You can do it here.

All you need to do is find a product that you love to recommend.

A company to promote that you trust and respect.

A dream bigger than your fears and frustrations.

And the rest is future in the making. Your future.

DARING GREATLY

"It is not the critic who counts: not the man who points out how the strong man stumbles or where the doer of deeds could have done better. The credit belongs to the man who is actually in the arena, whose face is marred by dust and sweat and blood, who strives valiantly, who errs and comes up short again and again, because there is no effort without error or shortcoming, but who knows the great enthusiasms, the great devotions, who spends himself for a worthy cause; who, at the best, knows, in the end, the triumph of high achievement, and who, at the worst, if he fails, at least he fails while daring greatly, so that his place shall never be with those cold and timid souls who knew neither victory nor defeat."

Theodore Roosevelt, 1858-1919
From the speech, Citizenship in a Republic, (Sorbonne, Paris; April 23, 1910)

THE MASTER GAME

"Seek, above all, for a game worth playing. Such is the advice of the oracle to modern man. Having found the game, play it with intensity— play as if your life and sanity depended on it (they do depend upon it). Follow the example of the French existentialists and flourish a banner bearing the word "engagement." Though nothing means anything and all roads are marked "No Exit," yet move as if your movements had some purpose. If life does not seem to offer a game worth playing, then invent one. For it must be clear, even to the most clouded intelligence, that any game is better than no game."

Robert S. DeRopp, 1913-1987
The Master Game, (Delacorte Press, 1968)

BLISS BUSINESS

Richard is also the author of *Mach II, The Art of Vision and Self Motivation*. This powerful work connects the Law of Attraction with the Laws of Action, teaching you exactly how to think, how to speak, how to feel and how to act in order to manifest your wildest Visions.

"I found a copy of **Mach II** at a friend's house. I read and loved it. So much of what the great athletes do to accomplish the impossible is done though visualization. Richard captures exactly how it works, why it works, and how anyone can use it to do great things in their life. Richard has a unique way of telling the story so we all really get it! I highly recommend this book to anyone wanting to master their own motivation and accomplishments."

John Elway
Super Bowl MVP & NFL Hall of Fame Quarterback

"Congratulations! Congratulations! Congratulations! Congratulations! Congratulations! I just read your **Mach II** book, and it is a masterpiece … head and shoulders above the rest of the motivation books I have read."

Harvey Mackay
Chairman & Founder, MackayMitchell

"In this accelerated economy you have to travel at **Mach II**. This book teaches you how to do it in an omni-effective and fun way."

Mark Victor Hansen
Co-creator, #1 New York Times Best-Selling series Chicken Soup for the Soul and Co-author, The One Minute Millionaire

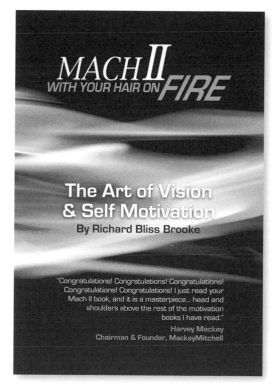

The Art of Vision
& Self Motivation
By Richard Bliss Brooke

"Congratulations! Congratulations! Congratulations!
Congratulations! Congratulations! I just read your
Mach II book, and it is a masterpiece... head and
shoulders above the rest of the motivation
books I have read."
Harvey Mackay
Chairman & Founder, MackayMitchell

"Absolutely incredible!"
John Addison
Co-CEO, Primerica

"I love **Mach II With Your Hair On Fire**.
I could tell when I read the book that Richard has a passion for changing people's lives. I respect Richard and his work and thank him for who he is and the difference and impact he's making in people's lives and businesses."

Les Brown
Motivational Speaker

Richard would love to hear your stories of how this work has impacted your life or business. You can reach Richard at 888.665.8484 or info@BlissBusiness.com.

You can order *The Four Year Career* (in either book, audio, and/or video formats) and *Mach II With Your Hair On Fire* at BlissBusiness.com